The Reflections Series: #1

Cracked Open

Reflections on the Transformative Power of Failure, Fear & Doubt

LESLIE K. MALIN, LCSW

Inquisitive Minds Press

©2016 Leslie K. Malin

All rights reserved. No part of this book may be reproduced, in any form, without written permission from the publisher.

Requests for permission to reproduce selections from this book should be mailed to:

Leslie Malin
Inquisitive Minds Press P.O. Box 52 , Saugerties, N.Y. 12477

Email: info@lesliemalinauthor.com

Published in the United States by Inquisitive Minds Press, an imprint of Alchemy of Aging, Leslie K. Malin LCSW, P.C.

ISBN 978-0-9975131-0-3

Book design by Austin Metze, www.metzedesign.com

Dedication

My deepest gratitude to all the teachers in my life—

My Parents,

Children,

Grandchildren,

Educators,

Healers,

Mentors,

Friends,

Clients,

Strangers,

Fellow Writers

And, the creative spirit

I am grateful ….

I am deeply grateful to the community of people who have so generously and lovingly supported me in creating and completing this book. Their belief, feedback and encouragement have been my ballast as I have navigated my way on this swelling sea of creation.

Thank you, Brenda Shoshanna who wrote the deeply moving Foreward. I have such respect for all you create and I am so honored by your beautiful words. (www.brendashoshanna.com)

And to Ashley Emma, who helped to edit this work and correct its grammar. It's not my strength! (www.ashleyemmaauthor.com)

To Austin Metze who designed the cover and so beautifully formatted the interior of this book. His warmth, generosity of spirit and commitment to this first-time author are deeply appreciated. (www.metzedesign.com)

Last but not least, a huge thank you for early readers of this book for their honest feedback and for cheering me on, as well as other wonderful friends who have been my constant champions, believing in me, even when I doubted myself.

Foreword

Brenda Shoshanna , Ph.D

Most of us spend our entire lives hiding from the deep, inner pain we feel. We have been trained to do so, taught to conform to an idealized image of who we are and how we must behave. The struggle between our essential reality and the idealized image we must live up to goes on endlessly. It destroys our peace, clouds our vision and turns what could be beautiful loving relationships into horrible power games. Over and over again we hear the refrain, "It all started out wonderfully; we were so happy. Then everything changed. Where has the love gone?"

In her powerful, extraordinary book *Cracked Open: Reflections on the Transformative Power of Failure, Fear & Doubt*, Leslie Malin plunges to the depth of this question: where have our love, courage, health and creativity gone when fear, failure, depression and doubt accost us? How do we navigate our way through this eternal struggle between forces of darkness and light?

In this book, the honesty, openness and vulnerability with which the author shares her journey, is both the path to healing and the message itself. "Words from the heart go into the heart" and the courage and strength expressed here will go into the reader's heart as well.

When hard times come, usually we close up, hunker down, and scramble for safety. We forget about the light within that is yearning to be expressed. We disregard the gifts we've been given that long to be shared. Few of us have the tools or understanding of how to navigate through these difficult times.

In this beautiful, fearless exploration of painful times, we realize that hiding from the darkness only makes it stronger. Our difficulties come with a gift in their hand. No need to hide from them at all. Better to mine the hidden treasures they offer.

As we face and claim our truth and are willing to take a new step that might have been frightening, a miraculous event often takes place. The darkness and difficulty transforms. The power of light, awareness and courage pours into our lives all by itself. We see the pain for what it was. And we see ourselves for what we truly are, as well.

Cracked Open inspires us to learn the lessons our sorrows have to teach. When we use difficulties as inspiration, we can become all that we are. We are then able to realize the enormous gifts and strength we have within and to taste the transformative power of light.

Essentially, this is a book about awakening. It is a book about claiming our truth, our courage and the incredible possibilities that life truly holds. It is about listening and trusting a different part of ourselves, taking back our power and living with the beauty and victory we always knew was right at our side.

Leslie Malin has embarked upon a rare and profound journey. Not only are we blessed to have her share it with us, but fortunate to be invited along on the journey as well. Enjoy each step of the way.

Brenda Shoshanna, a former practicing psychologist, is the author of many books that integrate Eastern and Western psychology and spirituality. Some of her books include, *Zen and the Art of Falling in Love*, *Zen Miracles* and she is presently working on a project called *Entering the Promised Land*. Discover more of her gifts at www.BrendaShoshanna.com.

> "There is a crack, a crack in everything.
> That's how the light gets in."
> —Leonard Cohen

Why This Book?

There is a burning question behind this book: "Can failure, fear and doubt alchemize us into deeper, more expansive and creative people?" Is it possible that these enemies to our well-being, never willingly sought, provide essential opportunities to release previously unknown strengths, birth surprising talents, and engender displays of unimaginable courage and authenticity?

Such questions arise, because I myself go through cycles of these psychic attacks and continue to be startled by the discovery of the gifts hidden within.

I am a lover of quotations. I have discovered that the "right" quotation can bring inspiration and emotional energy for digging deeper within myself. Quotations are questions pushing me to consider life through different prisms. This volume combines quotations from many traditions, eras, and genres of writers, coupled with my reflections on their meaning.

My reflections are grounded in my personal history, enriched by the scores of challenges and triumphs I have witnessed in the lives of my clients over more than a 35-year career as psychotherapist, coach, mentor and fellow traveler. My hope is that this book will read like a choral piece with a Question and a Responding Answer. Where it ultimately goes for you, I do not know; however, I hope it serves as a portal to new inner dimensions.

These quotations are prayers for illumination, a struck match in the darkness that exposes a space, previously unseen, and provides just enough light for us to move forward step by careful step. Life's triumphs over darkness are not measured by their velocity, but rather by faith, determination, and vision.

Dip into this volume, perchance to discover just the right words to challenge, inspire, and provide hope, courage and meaning. These words are a reminder that your life is waiting for you. You have what you need to take the next step. Beneath the cracks in the darkness rests the light.

A good friend had once wisely shared this piece of wisdom during a very challenging and frightening time in my life. She simply asked, "Can you make it to midnight?" I have used that very question for myself and others for many years. It has provided the courage and fortitude to hold on until the next dawn.

Introduction

Today I am in my 7th decade. This is shocking to me. Where did that time go? Portions of it feel like a dream – of both sweet and nightmare dimensions. I wonder, did I actually live it? I know I was there, but at times I feel more like an observer of my Self-in-Action and at other times the very much present actor on the stage.

Even as I write this book, I am puzzled by how it began. Where did the idea of it come from? From what pause in my life, heart and mind did it find a fertile resting place suitable to plant its roots, poke its head above the hardened earth, defiantly sprout its stalks and leaves and later burst into flower?

Such is the mystery of life. If we are honest, we don't know where the next creation comes from; we only know later, in retrospect, that it has occurred.

> "Today I affirm that I am divinely guided. There is that within that knows what to do and how to do it. And it compels me to act on what it knows."
>
> —Ernest Holmes

These decades have not passed without their joys and triumphs as well as their sorrows, disappointments and defeats. Yet, all of it, each scrap of life, has become an essential facet of my identity. Each has to be bowed down to in thanks and appreciation, especially the ugly parts. Those very life experiences I wish had passed my door as the angels of the Israelites passed over their doorways to visit devastation upon their oppressors. They, they are my mentors.

However, if there is one thing my own life has taught is that none of us goes forth in life unscathed. Darkness is one side of the coin of life and light is the other.

I have concluded that this is what life intends. Life brings illumination through its battles between the darkness and the light. As the clash of the Titans, when the force of steel on steel comes into our life-battle, our hero-selves can emerge.

We don't all emerge victorious. There are no guarantees of happy endings. However, I cannot face away from the darkness when it comes. And it does come, often when I feel least prepared. But somehow, at the point when I feel overcome, somehow my fool-hardy courage is summoned; a stone from my slingshot is released and I dare to face down the giant monster that awaits me, letting come what may come.

To letting the light in,

Leslie K. Malin, LCSW, ACSW

"We are all failures, at least the best of us are."

—James Barrie

When was it, I wonder, when we became so afraid?

Would a baby ever trust or love or smile?

Would she try to turn over or crawl or walk?

Would she try to speak or sing?

Does a toddler know that his scribbles look nothing like a flower? Does he care?

Would he build with blocks, only to see them tumble?

Would they attempt any of these things if fear were present?

When did I become so afraid?

When did you?

What shall we do about it?

"Until you try, you don't know what you can do."

—Henry James

Have you ever sat and daydreamed…

If only I could …

Paint like that,

Write a bestseller, Dance like the wind,

Create magic,

Inspire others, inspire myself,

Be love.

You don't know what you can do until you try.

"Being in the right place
at the right time
won't make you a success –
unless you're ready.
The important question is,
Are you ready?"

—Johnny Carson

I wonder. What is it to be ready?

Sometimes I'm all fired up and raring to go!
        And then, my enthusiasm exhausts me.   Plop.

Other times, I creep up on something.

Go at it sideways. A sleek cat stalking its prey, I silently tiptoe so as not to Startle it into flight, and it's gone.

But then, those quiet no-big-thing moments; I'm taken by surprise.
    Settled,   grounded,   peaceful,   not too excited,   not tentative,

No fireworks,   nor grand announcements,

I just know that I've landed. I'm ready. Perhaps it's the right place, the right time?

Maybe I will become a big success?

And suddenly I realize,
I care less about becoming a success; I care deeply that I have begun.

"What the caterpillar calls a tragedy, the master calls a butterfly."

—Richard Bach

If only I was equal to my imagination.

We are our own creation.
Often, more than we wish to acknowledge, we are dissatisfied, embarrassed, and ashamed of what we have created.

An imperfect version of my imaginings;
I find the Me of Me wanting;

                                        less than.

But we keep on. We persevere.

And, on one unremarkable day; something remarkable happens.

You discover your beauty.

"When everything is peaceful,
don't forget the danger;"
"When things are safe,
don't lose your edge —
A brittle thing can break

        easily

And a small thing fragment."

—Tao Te Ching, The New Translation
Man-Ho Kwok, Martin Palmer, Jay Ramsey

We can so easily be lulled into a sense of well-being – a complacency; a kind of hypnosis. I have been rocked in such a cradle, resting on such a bough, and it invariably falls – falls hard.

We can't grow, flourish, evolve or become unstuck unless we fight this hypnogogic drifting into unconsciousness.

It doesn't take soaring leaps or acts of flashy courage.

Rather, we dare the balancing from one mossy, slippery stone to another. Remember: the rocks are not boulders to deter us, but stepping stones leading the way.

"A journey of a thousand miles starts with the first step.
To act as if you know it all is catastrophic and if you try to control it,
you will stare into your empty hand."

Tao Te Ching, The New Translation

"Do you want it more than you are afraid of it?"

—Leslie Malin

Sometimes I find myself so afraid that I don't know I am afraid.
I think,

"Oh, I don't know enough yet —
I have to buy that new book, read that last article…
I'm too busy; what was I thinking?
Oops, I forgot to do the laundry."

Anything, other than to just start…

You just have to start.

One word at a time,

One brush stroke,

One less cookie;

One small decision in this moment can change everything.

"STAND UP. LOOK 'EM IN THE EYE AND TELL THEM WHAT YOU KNOW."

—Dan Rather

It takes guts,

It takes courage

To stand in the center of your being

and tell it like you see it,

like you know it,

like you feel it

AND

let come what may — come.

"Truly it is in the darkness
that one finds the light
so when we are in sorrow,
then this light is
nearest of all to us."

—Meister Eckhart

I have had my quotient of darkness, sorrow & confusion.
Times when I couldn't get out of bed,
so overwhelmed with anxiety
that I forgot it was possible to feel joy.

Times when those closest to me fled, abandoned;

Regaining my footing for the upward climb; courage, belief,
strength startle as they emerge on the horizon of the darkness.

Ahhh…

the light was always there
patiently waiting for me.

    Will I remember the light the next time darkness falls?

"You shall be free indeed
when your days are not
without a care,
Nor your nights without want
and a grief.
But rather when these things
girdle your life and yet
You rise above them naked
and unbound."

—Kahlil Gibran

I remember reading M. Scott Peck's words –

"Life isn't easy, it wasn't meant to be."

I was pretty young and untested by the world at that time, yet his words resonated with me. They made sense, even as they frightened me.

How can I discover my essence if there is nothing to push against?

How can I hone my skills, awareness, and character if there is nothing that terrifies?

How can I get to know myself or what I may be capable of, if life did not deliver hardship, shame, unhappiness, and defeat?

How often must I remind myself that freedom partners with grief, loss, fear and failure?

None of us opens the door to happily invite distress, want and grief to our table. They come unbidden.

What would I be without my uninvited guests?

"Courage does not always roar.
Sometimes courage
is the quiet voice at the
end of the day saying,
"I will try again tomorrow."

—Mary Anne Radmacher

I have been blessed with a series of clients who are my teachers on the nature of failure and the ephemeral substance of wellness:

Failure of the body or mind,
Failure of luck,
Failure of family;
Frequently facing a lifetime of struggle against
                immutable and declining circumstance.

Yet they persist —
Reach out,
Make jokes,
Smile,
Cry.

They write,   they study,   they work,   they love,
And try again — tomorrow, tomorrow & tomorrow.

*"Ring the bells that can still ring.
Forget your perfect offering.
There is a crack, a crack in everything.
That's how the light gets in."*

—Leonard Cohen

"Forget your perfect offering."

Have you ever noticed if you wait for perfection, your wait will be everlasting and your spirit will splinter?

Have you ever noticed how a little spark
of light in the darkness illuminates
an unexplored corner
vastly more than a floodlight ever could?

A spotlight in the darkened theater of your life
Can bring you *Alive*.

"Sometimes
Life seizes
Up
Nothing stirs
Nothing flows
We think:
All this time.
Climbing this
Rough tree
The rope
Attached
To
A rotten
Branch!
We think
Why did I choose
This path
Anyway?
Nothing at
The end
But sheer cliff
& Rock filled
Sea."

—ALICE WALKER,
EXCERPT FROM POEM *MY FRIEND YESHI*,
*WE ARE THE ONES WE HAVE BEEN WAITING FOR:
INNER LIGHT IN THE TIME OF DARKNESS*

Do you know this place,
Where nothing you do makes a ripple in time?
When you know you'd be more productive reading a thriller or watching the Food Network,
BECAUSE
        Nothing is happening.   Nothing can happen.
You strive to make progress against the storm's headwinds,
knowing that all effort is misspent and truly laughable.

Flash-frozen, held fast beneath the weight of a deep soul-freeze.
I know this place.
      I have been its captive.
I have escaped — for now. Somehow the ground thaws. Spring arrives.

"We are not
Over
When we think
We are."

—ALICE WALKER

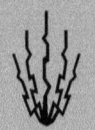

"When we fear things, I think we wish for them... Every fear hides a wish."

—David Mamet

Is that true? Do I really long for what I fear? What do I fear?
my terminal humanness,
my fragility,
my gifts,
my life's due date.

Do I really long for what I fear? How can that be?
Perhaps I don't wish for those things,
perhaps I wish for what may lie beneath.

Perhaps I yearn for the strength aroused when my fear comes forth
to challenge me, mano a mano.
Perhaps I yearn for the success that fear denies me.
Perhaps I crave the proof that I can vanquish my demons yet again.

    You see, I know full well that demons are immortal.

"Making your mark in the world is hard. If it was easy everyone would do it. But it's not. It takes patience; it takes commitment, and it comes with plenty of failure along the way. The real test is not whether you avoid this failure, because you won't. It's whether you let it harden or shame you into inaction, or whether you learn from it, whether you choose to persevere."

—Barack Obama, Speech on July 12, 2006

Making our mark on the world doesn't need to be a BIG Thing.

It's most often the small, unremarked gesture, action, thought or phrase that resounds through time.

That almost unobserved act serves to change a person's feeling, rescues them from despair, provides hope where before there was defeat, applauds strengths and gifts rather than deliver ridicule and diminishment.

Making a mark, big or small requires an intention, an abiding desire to make a difference.
Making a mark on the world demands that we show up, no matter the odds for success.

The world is begging, *Show- Up!*

In the first days, the question–
"Why are you here?"
"Don't know really."
Yet with unquestioned certainty I've been led here by
A gentle, insistent hand.
"Why now?"
Because it's time,
Time to move more swiftly through bittersweet letting-go's.
Time to evict ancient tenants clutching fiercely to long
Expired leases.
Time to cleanse my home of toxic waste dumped by
False prophets, prior lives, other people's lies, child-totem beliefs,
All that weeps.
Companions too long protected, cherished.
Yet, I am an expert on the
Tenderness, fragility, and life expectancy of new beginnings.
Demon spirits recently made homeless lurk in the shadow-lands,
Confidently waiting,
All packed up and ready to move back in.
Waiting for my vision to crumble,
My faith to collapse.

—LESLIE K. MALIN, WRITTEN AT THE ARTIST WAY IN TAOS, NEW MEXICO

Our workshop leader was not showing up…

Reason? Cloudy.

This week was to be led by others. Many attendees left.

Not me.

I was supposed to be there.

Something unknown was waiting for me,

a part of myself previously unmet.

I wrote this first-ever poem there.

it arrived unbidden, unannounced.

One minute I was uncertain if I would even try to

write a poem – much less read it to the group;

the next moment, it appeared in my notebook.

Where did it come from?

I don't know. But it felt like a Gift.

Sometimes the most meaningful,

unexpected treasures appear

when we decide to make an appearance as well.

"Sorrow happens, hardship happens; the hell with it, who never knew the price of happiness will not be happy."

—Yevgeny Yevtushenko

I was shocked when I happened upon this.
I had to read it many times
to get it — to understand, to submit to its truth.
Moving through childhood I knew this truth.
A friend I thought loved me
deserts me in the playground for a brighter shining star
than my own.
I am desolate, inconsolable, crushed.
In the next moment,
I look up and someone I had not noticed before,
someone I had been blind to, asks me to join in.
I move forward, discarding my pain
like a gum wrapper.
At what point did I begin to believe in my
entitled immunity from sadness?
Is arrogance a defense against the certainty that
every joy has an underbelly of loss and pain, that
every triumph holds the antecedents of defeat?

"One day
in the middle of my life,
I awakened in a dark wood
where the true way was
totally lost."

—Dante Aligerheri

I have awakened in such a place. One moment I was walking in the sunlight through my life, certain I knew who I was, what I was doing, where I was going, and then —

Darkness surrounded. I had no idea where I was, or how I had arrived in that place.

It wasn't depression. At that time, I wasn't a familiar of that darkness. It was a shocked-into-paralysis, stranger-than-fiction lostness, yet absent of fear.

I was fully present, possibly for the first time – In the Now.

No Past; no Future; no Plan; no Strategy to get me out.

A here-one-moment, gone-the-next ash entombed citizen of Pompeii.

Some time had passed, buried in the dead zone, when

A friend inquires, "What are you doing about this?"

"I'm listening."

"For what?" she asked.

"*I don't know right now,*

But I am confident that I will hear it when I am ready."

At that exact moment I discovered that Faith was my silent, constant companion.

ॐ

"PEACE.
It does not mean to be in a place where there is no noise, trouble or hard work. It means to be in the midst of those things and still be in the calm of your heart."

—Author Unknown

People come to work with me to fix their problems.

    Not to "fix" themselves.

We each come into therapy with a secret, even to ourselves —

    The Secret Plea: "Rid me of my problems, but "don't ask me to change".

    Change is difficult. Change is uncomfortable. Change has an unknown and fickle outcome. Change does not ensure a happy ending.

    The most powerful healing is finding your way to your Silent Center where patiently, seated in lotus position

              your Soul resides.

Regardless of the tumult that swirls and the confusion that jangles our nerves, at our center is a kind and gentle knowing presence patiently awaiting our arrival.

        I can't get there all the time, or even some of the time.

           However, often, just trusting that it exists

                as surely as my heart beats,

      gives me enough courage to wait out the storm.

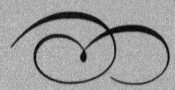

"Our greatest challenge is to make our very own
Home in the world.
When we stand apart from ourselves, or
When we stand with others,
Who don't stand with or for us,
We die a little every day."

—Leslie Malin

You better watch out, it's a slow frog-in-the-boiling-water kind of death, lulled into unconsciousness by an incremental rising of the flame. It's a freezing-to-death-in-the-snow-until sleep snuffs out your life.

Jump Out!
Wake Up!
Fight for your aliveness!
Stand alone if that's what it takes,
But take the stand.
Sure, you're afraid.
But when did staying in fear ever get you anywhere you wanted to be?
Everything awaits you. Everything is waiting for you.
What exactly are you waiting for?
Have we always been so uncomfortable in the space of unknowing?
We become anxious with the undefined quiet, the uninhabited space where we believe knowing and certainty should abide.

"I said to my soul, be still, and wait without hope, for hope would be hope for the wrong thing: wait without love, for love would be love for the wrong thing; there is yet faith. But the faith and the love and the hope are all in the waiting."

—T.S. Eliot

We feel less-than when answers are not readily available. Ashamed to be deserted by the facile answer, the snap-in-place Lego decision, and we get anxious.

We scrunch up, become reactively hyperactive, breath comes fast and shallow; palms sweat, the heart palpates; the mind, a carnival of flashing lights, carnival barker's shouts, and enticing smells that deliver emptiness.

We grasp at the smoke of unlikely resolution. We cry out at the injustice. We flail about, trying to convince ourselves that our very striving proves us worthy.

We become our own avenging judge, jury, and guard of our imprisonment.

Stop struggling.   Cease spinning.   Go quiet.

Everything emerges from the unseen alive space
between words, breaths, heartbeats.

Be still, wait.
After all, do you really have another choice?

> "Last night, as I was sleeping
> I dreamt — marvelous error! —
> that I had a beehive
> here inside my heart.
> And the golden bees
> were making white combs
> and sweet honey
> from my old failures."
>
> —Antonio Machado
> translated by Robert Bly

It has been said that nothing in life is wasted, that the universe has no spare parts. That everything happens for a reason, even if we can't grasp it from our current place of understanding.

I repeat the same aphorisms. Am I perpetrating a fraud on myself, on others?

But here is what I know for sure…

At any unexpected moment transformative, miraculous, unperceived parts of ourselves can be birthed from our failures, our defeats, and our shame, together capable of life-rescue.

Trust these unlikely Sherpa; let them lead you safely down from the cliffs of your Himalayan terror.

The trek can be tortuous, and will challenge your faith, its progress only noted in retrospect, so indirect the route.

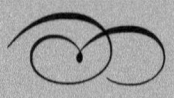

"Life is either a daring
adventure or nothing.
To keep our faces toward change
and behave like free spirits
in the presence of fate
is strength undefeatable."

—Helen Keller

There is rarely a client who hasn't asked, "How do you listen to people all day? Don't you get tired, bored? Don't you ever think, God, this person is hopeless?'

These are pleas for acceptance; a get-out-of-jail-free card that arrives at the very moment when someone actually hears his own repetitive and lifeless narrative. It takes time, so much time, to hear our inner voice and… submit to its truth.

As a hunting vulture, we circle our fears, self-doubts and shame, waiting to feel safe enough to land and feast on the dead. For most, becoming a "free spirit in the presence of fate" takes a lifetime of effort.

We try to hide from fate and change. We cower in the darkness of our terrified hearts.

Salvation lies in throwing ourselves onto the path of our fear. Only there can we claim our freedom and strength.

"A PERSON WILL
BE CALLED ON
JUDGMENT DAY
FOR EVERYTHING
PERMISSIBLE
HE COULD HAVE
ENJOYED
AND DID NOT."

—Talmud

I can find myself on a free weekend sitting at my computer and working.

Rather than taking those priceless moments, ones that will never come my way again, to seek enjoyment, entertainment, leisure, a good spy novel or the company of friends and family.

It's not that I never take time for myself. It's that I can feel guilty or uneasy. I overhear myself apologizing for vacations, meandering weekends.

I must believe that I have to earn my pleasures, pay for "time off".

Now I know that's upside down.

I understand that there is a difference between work supporting my life and letting my life become synonymous with work. So, knowing this, why do I sometimes withhold enjoyment or take it only in small, measured doses?

If you are angry with yourself, feel that you have fallen from your ideal self, are not earning the money you used to, don't have the job you have the skill for, you are still entitled to enjoyment, laughter, play, creativity and time with those you love .

Enjoyment is our birthright. It gives color to our lives. It leaves space for creativity to enter.

"When the aching sense of the disjointedness in ourselves becomes acute enough we anxiously reach out to find the elixir of wholeness."

—Leslie Malin

Some look into the mirror of love desperate to see their reflected perfection in the eyes of the beloved.
Others look to the bottle,
The pill,
The needle,
Praying to experience a reunion of self, or more accurately, a celebration of our illusory belief in the possibility of wholeness.

What if we could embrace the notion that
The empty spaces within,
The pauses between,
are a resting place,
a breath,
a giver of life, not a killer of souls?

Isn't a cup defined as much by its tangible shape as by the emptiness it holds?

"Don't ask yourself what the world needs;
Ask yourself what makes you come alive
and then go do it.
Because what the world needs is people
who have come alive."

—H. Thurman

Most of us are so distanced from our inner being that we don't have a glimmer of an idea what makes us tingle with delight, fall in love with an idea, or go daft over a glimpse of a person's profile as they get off the bus.

We have become scanners of the exterior and tone deaf to our interior.

We fret over what job titles, activities, clubs, or volunteer work will set us apart on our resumes, our academic applications, or posted to online job boards that we have totally forgotten who we are, or ever were to ourselves.

Forget emotion! Feelings are distractions! Joy is for the few, or maybe just a myth made up to make us feel empty and despondent.

What's real is what the world demands, what unfilled gap in the universe we can fill. What new activity, store, concept or technology will make us seen? Make us famous? Make us rich? Make us real?

Perhaps the reason that most everything in current culture feels so empty is that we don't inhabit the space. We don't occupy ourselves.

What will it take to find the courage to safari into our inner darkness with only a fool's expectation of bringing forth the diamond of hope?

"The essence of life is that it's challenging. Sometimes it is sweet, and sometimes it is bitter… From an awakened perspective, trying to tie up all the loose ends and finally get it put together is death, because it involves rejecting a lot of your basic experience. There is something aggressive about that approach to life, trying to flatten out all the rough spots and imperfections into a nice smooth ride."

—Pema Chödron
When Things Fall Apart: Heart Advice for Difficult Times

"...Trying to tie up all the loose ends and finally get it put together is death."

Such a kick-in-the-belly statement, but true. How often have I longed for a seamless life; I imagine it as a smooth sail on a glassy sea, a hammock ride of a life, a graceful swaying on gentle breezes kind of life.

And then, of course, I throw in a hand grenade and scatter the picturesque pieces all over the place. Kaboom… That's the aggressive approach I seem to prefer. I dance under the confetti falling, rather than choosing to sleep beneath the beautiful frozen perfection of stillness. Here's to the power of disruption over the safety of tidiness!

Here's the thing: I don't crave chaos. I abhor the anxiety that electrifies me when I feel out of control. It frightens and shakes me. I can feel guilty and even ashamed when I make a mess of things. I often look over my shoulder at my life choices and shake my head in disbelief… What the hell?

So, the way of my life is really a paradox. And I, its central character, will probably not really ever understand it, even at its inevitable end.

What I know is that is how I am made. Maybe I am more afraid of a death-like life than a jagged and rough cut one. Believe me, this doesn't make me any poster child for the right way to live a life. I am not advocating this for you.

But here is one thing I do advocate – and that's Living Your Life. Don't let your life die on the curb of safety, fear, and unlived aspirations. Challenge your belief that your value is equivalent to how smoothly you row your boat. Get out into the deep waters some times. It's there that your strength and mastery will emerge.

"Whatever the present moment contains, accept it as if you had chosen it. Always work with it, not against it."

—Eckhart Tolle

One of the most beautiful sights is watching how a master martial artist works with the energies and forces that are presented in the exact moment they find themselves in.

I marvel at how they seem to welcome the resistance, embrace the opposing force as an opportunity to engage rather than as a threat to their being.

As they respond, they appear in flow, learning about themselves as they learn about the other.

I don't know what they are feeling inside of themselves.

I am certain that there can be fear, threats, perhaps anger, but each of those inner adversaries bends to their will as they practice and perfect their craft.

They are warriors of a special order. Even if they are overcome by the opposing force; there are no losers. There is no shame.

They have met the present moment. They have chosen it.

"Listen to your life. See it for the fathomless mystery that it is. In the boredom and pain of it, no less than the excitement and gladness; touch, taste, smell your way to the holy and hidden heart of it, because in the last analysis, all moments are key moments and life itself is grace."

—Frederick Buechner

"Listen to your life"

How many of us want to do that? When what we so often repeat are the reverberations of our perceived failures, losses and agonies going back over the years, over the decades, perhaps over the millennia. Listen to the stories we tell: "My mother was alcoholic. My father deserted us. I wasn't loved enough. I wasn't encouraged, I was, I wasn't." We all have our stories, stories that have taken on the power of myth; morphing into unalterable truths that define what we believe is possible in our Now.

Stories that we use to excuse ourselves, to judge ourselves, to limit ourselves, to blame others, to explain failure away, to lower expectations (ours and others), hoping that the telling of them will change the trajectory of our lives and ultimately excuse us when we fail to show up in this moment, in the now.

But here's the thing, all those stories, they are our allies in waiting, our arrows pointing inwards to a vital vision of life that is always waiting to be unwrapped.

Shuck off those oyster shell stories of ugliness, roughness, and grayness and open to the tender beauty and deliciousness waiting inside to be tasted, savored, and desired.

You are the person you have been waiting for. Listen to your life "the holy and hidden heart of it" where "life itself is grace".

"The antidote to lack is gratitude. Gratitude is a choice, an attitude, an approach towards life. My gratitude for this moment does not depend on what is going on in the moment; it is the moment regardless of what is going on, that I am grateful for. My gratitude for this breath is not about the breath. It's that I am breathing, that I recognize that it comes from a higher source and that I am alive. Gratitude is a moment-to-moment celebration."

—JOHN-ROGER

As much as I would love to exist in the ongoing flow of gratitude, I can only glimpse that for small moments, snippets of time. When I can, it's not that I am unaware of problems, challenges, or unhappy places that populate my life, but they are in the background: they become sepia-toned as in an old photograph, and they fail to take me over.

When I welcome the moment as all that counts, when I realize that I am still here, finding my way, when I allow myself to take in that I am supported, even if I have no idea of how, why or what that actually means, then I can welcome the sense of being held by a source beyond my understanding.

I have been given the gift of life, that life is often messy, unpleasant, frightening, sad, lonely, as well as joyous, triumphant, tender, and awesome. Each breath comes in one moment, is suspended in a gap and then let go, awaiting the next breath to carry me, to where I know not.

Most of us hold our breath throughout our lives. I often do the same.

I fail to celebrate, despite whatever challenges, doubts, and fears may encircle me, that I am alive!

In any moment I may turn the corner and take my thoughts, feelings and life in another direction. How can I be so ungrateful for such a gift?

"What is needed, rather than running away or controlling or suppressing or any other resistance, is understanding fear; that means watch it, learn about it, come directly into contact with it. We are to learn about fear, not how to escape from it."

—Jiddu Krishnamurti

I wish I could tell you proudly that when I am afraid, I am always courageous. Truth be told, I can't always rest into the panic that arises when I feel fear approaching.

I have gotten better though. I have learned some strategies, discovered some helpful meditations, as well as other techniques that help me slow my breathing, put the pieces of my mind back in order, and challenge the fear and its truthfulness when it demands that I believe just what it tells me.

Things I have learned about my fear when I can stand my ground and stare back into its monstrous face, is that…

Fear starts from a grain of truth but it quickly outpaces that truth so that it appears bigger, stronger; more important. Fear wants to be omnipotent. It wants to rule me, to take me over, to loom fearsomely above me as I am prostrate.

Fear depends upon my not knowing my own strength. Fear wants to overpower my ability to listen, to obscure truth from fiction.

Yet, here's the ironic thing: Fear thinks it is saving me, protecting me, keeping me safe from harm.

My job is to assure it that I hear its warnings and that, unless body and soul are really at risk, that I am now a grown-up and I can learn from my fear and not be taken over by it.

I welcome fear — my teacher, my guide, my way out as well as my way in.

"Our goal should be to live life in radical amazement…get up in the morning and look at the world in a way that takes nothing for granted. Everything is phenomenal… To be spiritual is to be amazed."

—Rabbi Abraham Joshua Heschel

"...To be Spiritual is to be Amazed"

I sit at my table and look at my computer when outside my window is the purest white, silver snow falling gently over the hill that descends to my home.

The blue tinge on the white snow that falls upon it at dusk, the branches of bushes and small trees that reach out for the sun and sky, challenging the snow to try and smother its desire, all this glory. The smooth untrammeled surface of the snow covers life beneath that receives the gift from above. And I? I get irritated!

"Aargh, another day like this!" Ugh, the roads are a mess! Oh, no, I have to shovel again." Such a spoiled brat I am, inured to the startling beauty that is showing off for me, so ungrateful for the peace that descends on such a day as today.

But now I listen, I strain to hear sounds from outside, but every bird is closed in tight and still. There is no howling wind. Everyone is huddling inside; no sounds of children laughing, cars moving, nor of life moving forward.

There's just me and the silent symphony of the floating, falling, incandescent snowflakes, each one pristine and offering itself for my pleasure.

Once the flakes fall, they will lose their perfect uniqueness. But for now, they remind me that I, as well, am a manifestation of the mystery, and also unique.

This moment I live in radical amazement!

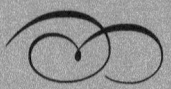

"Many people go through life accomplishing nothing because they are unwilling to do anything for fear of making a mistake. There is no need to be afraid of mistakes or even of failures. Any mistakes which may be made by a person who is obedient to the still small voice will be few, and they will not be irretrievable; he can quickly pick himself up again and soon be wholly immersed in the spirit. Mistakes are not fatal, not one is forever: success is forever, but failure is only for a day."

—Joel S. Goldsmith
   Practicing the Presence

When did we get so inside out, where Fear is the outside garment that zips up our spirit? Fear blocks our trusting the inevitability of ongoing possibility. Fear comes like a gangster, threatening us, imposing on us that we need the protection that only it, fear, can offer.

Fear tries to eradicate the truth.

Only moving forward and casting off that garment of fear, anxiety and panic can make us whole. Only then can we come fully alive and heal our wounded hearts.

We live 'tight in the bud' and while this is painful and stifling, we have misinterpreted the pain as safety, as wisdom perhaps, as level-headed caution and acts of prudence. It's none of those things.

We are not meant to curve in upon ourselves, nor drive down our courage, faith, curiosity, and willingness to fall and rise, rise and fall. failure is in a moment, not a lifetime.

Failure is never getting off our knees to stand in the sun — exposed and ready to be seen as the perfectly imperfect people we are.

I am imperfect. I am a beginner at life, regardless of the years I've lived. I mess up. I shame myself. I let myself down. I pull myself up. So what? When I am able to show up in my life this way, I become alive. I am real. I am free. And, now, at last, I am beginning to understand that this is really enough — that showing up is the blessing.

I don't want to go into my death having let fear kill me in life.

"True understanding is to see the events of life in this way: 'You are here for my benefit, though rumor paints you otherwise. And everything is turned to one's advantage when he greets a situation like this. You are the very thing I was looking for. Truly whatever arises in life is the right material to bring about your growth and the growth of those around you. This, in a word, is art — and this art called 'life' is a practice suitable to both men and gods. Everything contains some special purpose and a hidden blessing; what then could be strange or arduous when all of life is here to greet you like an old and faithful friend."

—Marcus Aurelius

The Last of the Five Good Emperors (Rome) Meditations

I work hard to remember, to reconnect the parts of the truth that tell me that "whatever arises in my life is the right material to bring about my growth".

Look, I'm no spiritual guru or prophet. I'm just like you: a person wrestling with life on life's terms and hoping to find the gift within the struggle, the pain, the confusion, the disappointment and the failure.

I used to believe that thinking like everything that arrives is an unexamined gift was a pie-in-the-sky, sunny-side-up way of being. It is not. What it is, is the key to everything.

When I become a child (that is at least several times a week!), I get angry and stamp my foot, demanding that life should be fair. Fair means that life should go my way, should be a gentle rocking-on-the-seas kind of experience, or a sky-rockets-in-flight event.

I secretly believe that, at those times, when life is being with-holding and mean, it behaves this way because I have done something wrong. I am not good enough, don't work hard enough, am not worth enough to have life's riches delivered at my door, red-ribbon clad.

However, when my more adult self shows up, I know that those beliefs are lies and distortions.

Every day the lesson arrives. I only grow when life pushes me in the direction of out-sizing my shell; when it casts me onto a land where I am a stranger without a compass, without a backpack, without a plan.

Each heartbreak, each defeat, even each resistance that I erect is my teacher in life. In order to more closely approach the person I was sent here to be, I have to find the silver lining in each storm (many of my own making). I am the one I am waiting for and it's time for me to arrive!

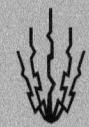

"The wounds
are the place
where the light
enters you."

—Rumi

Once again, wisdom informs me that my wounds are the places that offer me the opportunity to see the light of my own being. Only when I dare being wounded do I receive the fruits of knowledge, self-discovery and inner strength.

It's not that we should choose situations that will bring us pain. Life has its own FedEx for bringing us broken pieces, failed expectations and nightmares.

But it is my choice, your choice, how we receive those deliveries. I can either caterwaul about the unfairness of life, about how it's too hard to deal with, what a victim I am. Or, I can sit with my woundedness and see what it has to teach me.

Having been around the block many times with such boo-boos to my spirit, I have become less squeamish about looking at them directly and not averting my eyes.

And, here's the astonishing thing: when I dare to look at my rawness, I can find a small center of wholeness, beauty and enlightenment. A new awareness dawns, a clarity emerges. And, because that light has come through; it has made me less afraid of the blows that may come as well.

Being less afraid lessens the anxiety and reminds me that I've been here before, will be again and that it's not only survivable, but can even be liberating and generative. Just to be clear… This doesn't mean that I am healed. But I am getting closer.

"Your task
is not to seek for love,
but merely to seek and
find all the barriers
within yourself that
have built against it."

—Rumi

Love in abundance surrounds us, but it won't just arrive at our door and beg to come in, (even though I so wish it worked that way!).

Love is an inside-out kind of thing. And it begins with me being able to love myself.

How frequently do we raise our fist and proclaim the injustice of it all – others are loved, others find their mate, their comfort, their safety.

Or we feel sorry for ourselves because we are "not worthy enough", "smart enough", "beautiful enough", "enough of enough" to be embraced by love. Then we are the victim of lovelessness, and we can look intensely for the parent, circumstance, or experience that had robbed us of our enoughness, our value.

However, I have come to believe that as long as we keep our not-enoughness so closely held, we can't love ourselves much less anyone else — and others can't give us enough love to make up for our lack.

And, when I don't love myself, no amount of love that I am surrounded by is accessible to me. There is no room in my heart. My heart is too buttressed by my hurts, my fears, my angers, and my resentments to allow love to penetrate my defenses.

And, paradoxically my defense system keeps me safe from the fearsomeness and vulnerability that authentic love requires of me.

Do we love our not-enoughness more than we hunger for love?

Are we, am I, willing to bring down the barriers and walk out emotionally naked and unarmed to greet the possibility of love?

"Whatever hurts you blesses you."

—Rumi

How do we receive blessings from our wounds? What is a blessing, anyway?

A blessing is something quiet, hushed and oft times long unnoticed. It is often only in retrospect that I recognize the gift.

A blessing is a gift that is bequeathed unto me, a richness that becomes part of my life, my awareness, my very being.

Blessings don't come with trumpets blasting more frequently they follow a descent into the darkened corners of my psyche and heart. It's in the heartache that blessings can arrive without warning and often stubbornly denied.

The blessing is the clearing that sometimes comes after I embrace my woundedness. It's the release from fighting against the shadows that are always lurking. It's the opportunity to accept the truth, even if it's beat up, scabbed and bruised

"Darkness is your candle."

—Rumi

I am like many. I can be blind to what treasures may lie in a dark alcove of my life when my life seems to be going well.

After all, things are good; why risk turning it upside down looking for trouble? Why not just embrace the shiny coin version of my life? What fool would not do that?

ME. I am often that fool.

Perhaps I have been at the introspection, self-inquiry gig for so long that I don't know another way of being. Do I make problems for myself? Probably.

However, problems, frustrations, people that drive me crazy, they are an unshakeable part of my life. I have learned that wallowing in self-deception and lack of inquiry only ends up biting me hard.

When I seize darkness as my candle, I am led to new discoveries. Sometime they are not pleasant and I have to wrestle them into submission. Yet, it can be just as possible that I find that I am living in a world too small for my soul. My vision is limited by my complacency.

Then, I need to brush up against the razor sharp coral to find out what's calling to me, what's trying to emerge.

The answers exist outside the problem, beyond the darkness. However, the problem and the darkness provide the light to climb upwards to discover what's waiting for me.

"Ever tried. Ever failed.
No matter. Try again.
Fail Again. Fail better."

—Samuel Beckett

Failure thrusts us into our vulnerable, undefended, blind side. And, by doing so places us in the field of all possibility.

My greatest possibilities, opportunities, growing edges have been birthed from my bitterest, most embarrassing and sometimes most public failures. Frequently these failures and falls from grace are small in the eyes of others and yet huge to me. Other times they've been blockbusters.

I've had businesses fail, incomes dissolve, friendships devolve, and those I believed loved me deliver unanticipated and unspeakable pain. Yet I've survived and, more importantly, keep learning.

It's not because I am so strong. I have slowly learned through the pain points that there are lessons awaiting my arrival: lessons about living life raw that only failure and pain can teach.

Loss and fear have right sized me and fostered my growth. How else would I have learned these lessons if someone told me how to finesse the hard times? I wouldn't have listened – would you?

I can't give you the formula for surviving what can feel unsurvivable. Your formula for navigating the unknown resides inside of you. You'll find it, lose it, and find it again. It's a hide-and-seek kind of thing.

"Fail. Fail Again. Fail Better."

"Forget safety.
Live where you
fear to live.
Destroy your
reputation. Be
notorious."

—Rumi

We all want to feel safe. Safety is a myth. I've discovered that I am most safe when I am able to see that I am always at risk.

When I can really embrace the reality that life, like the very ocean can throw me waves that drag me under and that I can either become one lost at sea or I can fight for my emergence and keep moving forward – then I can be more secure.

It's strange how security and randomness can coexist.

Now, I can't always be so zen-like and accepting, but I am much better at surfing the waves and finding my way in the dark.

You see, I know the sea will calm. And, I know there is only dark where light exists. I've become better at breathing through the pain and not holding my breath when pain, assuredly and without anticipation, arrives.

No one. No one. No one has a lifetime exemption from pain, loss, fear and doubt. I knew a very wealthy man who acted as if life couldn't touch him. He believed, he really believed that his abundance was a shield of protection, that it inured him from grief and loss. He had no patience for the emotional struggles of life, nor empathy for the strugglers. That is until his son died from an overdose. I don't know if he has gained any insight or deepening of feelings for others, but he is bent over from his pain and perhaps from his awareness that he was a participant in the unfolding of this tragedy.

Life comes but with one guarantee and that is failure, fear and doubt are always cruising the neighborhood ready to deliver a whip lashing to the soul.

How you respond to the assault can make or break you.

"I have lived
on the lip of insanity,
wanting to
know reasons,
Knocking on the door,
It opens;
I've been knocking
from the inside."

—Rumi

Is it easier for you to hold onto pain and lack of forgiveness than in the sweet surrender of letting go?

After years working on this phenomenon, I've gained some new skills. I have wrestled with the issue of forgiveness and recognize that when I hold onto my anger and disappointment the only person harmed is I — the other person is totally untouched by my grievances. The world owes me nothing. Other people, regardless of our relationship or what we may have been to each other owe me anything. It is really about what I owe myself.

When I sabotage myself I am the source of being unloving. When I resist or pull away from engaging my gifts or claiming my power, I am the barrier to my evolution.

Rather than hate those inner saboteurs, I work to engage them in dialogue to discover the lessons they yearn to teach. It's hard work to release judgment and anger allowing the potential for a lasting letting go.

"You were born with wings. Why prefer to crawl through life?"

—Rumi

I am now what young people call "old".
I am what some may say is unsuccessful.
I am what others may see as always searching, playing hide and seek with my life.
I am what critics may judge as opinionated, stubborn, believer in things not yet seen,
I am closer to the end of my life, yet feel still like a beginner at life.

I say, I am what I am. And, that's all right.
I call myself wise.
I call myself burnished by the exigencies of life.
I call myself a survivor and a rescuer, a teacher and a student.
I am lost and found.
I am a living contradiction – I soar and I crawl.
I am resilient and intractable.
And, finally, what I am and what I may still become is a wonderment to me.
Life has taken me far and wide, but here I am, on this page, at this moment in my life, and what will be will be, but not without my having a say in it!

"You are not a drop in the ocean. You are the ocean in a drop."

—Rumi

You are not a cutoff, dismembered part of the whole, even if you believe you are. In you is me, us, them, the moon and the stars, the galaxies and the dark holes.

In you are Moses, Christ, Buddha, Mohammad, the terrorist, the criminal, the insane, the homeless and the wrecked.

Your sense of separateness is an illusion. And, that illusion may well be killing your spirit; robbing you of hope, cobbling your dreams and drowning you in fear.

You have everything within you that can birth your own version of perfection. No, you are not the sun — you are a beam of its light varying in color, intensity, and duration.

I've finally come to realize that I am not the source of whatever I create, be it great or ghastly, I am a reflection, a version, a beam of the source and that's my purpose, just to be the beam. It's your purpose as well.

We are each here for a fraction of time; let's live life like the sun, capable of destruction yes, yet a source of life, amazement, and endless possibility. You have inherited that legacy, so let yourself shine in whatever way you can.

The small wonderment is no less than the shooting star.

"Dance when you're broken open;
Dance if you've torn the bandage off;
Dance in the middle of fighting;
Dance in your blood;
Dance when you're perfectly free."

—Rumi

"Dance when you're broken"! I should dance when pain, shame, rejection, and my smallness seeps through the cracks of my smooth, seemingly unspoiled veneer? Yes, I should dance!

I should dance to prove that I have survived.

Dance as my defiance when faced with defeat.

Dance despite exposed, bleeding wounds as I wander in a battlefield; dance because I still can.

Dance because whatever has occurred is occurring yet I am still ～～ here. That's worth dancing for.

I always have to remind myself that:

Even when I fall short;

Even when I feel wounded;

Even when I shudder from fear when chaos surrounds, I am still ～～here! I am alive!

I can change my thoughts, my habits, and my actions because I have been taught new lessons about what doesn't work, as well as what I must change or understand differently and that is being "perfectly free". Perfectly free to dance.

"Be soft. Do not let the
world make you hard.
Do not let the pain
make you hard.
Do not let the bitterness
steal your sweetness.
Take pride that even
though the rest of
them may disagree,
You still believe it to be a
beautiful place."

—Kurt Vonnegut

Is it because I am in my elder years that I perceive the world as an increasingly disorienting and unwelcoming place? Retrospect is often covered by the soft misty fog of remembrance. However, looking in the rearview mirror of my life and then turning to face the present, I can't help but mourn the loss of our innocence, the diminution of hope, or the departure of grace.

It demands a sustained and vigilant fight to remain soft in the face of so much pain, ours and the pain of the world. Many believe that to become steely is the only path to survival. Yet, they fail to calibrate the price of committing such a magnitude of emotional resources to such an undertaking.

Heed the warnings: Retrieving softness and sweetness after the armoring of hearts and souls may not be an option, as the capacity for self-compassion and compassion for others may have been forfeited.

How I choose to act, speak and participate determines the core of my world. In that moment when I can reach out my hand, not pull away in anticipatory fear of the sharp slap that may come, I have defeated bitterness and mistrust.

And since I can only live moment by moment, that has to be enough.

"To find your peace,
you have to let your armor go;
your need for acceptance
can make you invisible in this world.
Risk being seen in all your glory."

—Jim Carrey, Actor
Graduation Address at Maharishi University

We are all born with a need for acceptance, nurturing and caring — it's called survival.

Yet somewhere along life's continuum such a "need" can become contaminated and transform to a poison.

When we live in fear that we are not enough, our courage can desert us.

When we buy the false prophet's cry that we need to take cover and hide our essential being because it is not sufficiently beautiful or worthy of respect, we sacrifice our sense of safety in the world.

When we hide away in an airless attic or in the deeply cold underground to escape those we fear will expose us, humiliate us, and ultimately exterminate us because they judge us deviant, we go dark. Our inner light goes out. We join the ranks of the living dead. Our essence becomes invisible.

Is the risk of "being seen in all your glory" so terrifying that you will choose the cloak of invisibility? It's a choice. And, it's yours alone.

"Our duty, as men and women, is to proceed as if limits to our ability did not exist."

—Chinese Fortune Cookie

When a truth comes wrapped in the stale, crusty shell of a Chinese fortune cookie from your local takeout, you know you need to sit up a little straighter and take notice!

Duty is defined as: "Something that you must do because it is morally right." Not just a good idea, more than a responsibility, greater than an obligation, it is a moral imperative

Duty propels us forward as if there is nothing to stop us. To "proceed as if limits to our ability did not exist" is to be propelled by inspiration salted with a touch of madness. It suggests that it is immoral when we fail to believe that each of us has something unique to give the world that it can't get without us.

Duty does not imply that we can't fail, or trip and stumble, nor only be considered successful when doing great and fame deserving things. It tells us that we have a duty to keep on keeping on, regardless of the outcome.

The journey is frequently the gift the faith walk provides. The outcome is not guaranteed nor is your worth measured by it. The world needs your courage, determination, and heroism and you need the same for yourself.

"You don't get more courage; you learn to do it afraid."

—Jeff Goins

I have faced many things in my life both super-sized and minuscule, I considered myself as having achieved a state of courageousness. "I am a courageous woman," I would think. Friends would commend and envy me for my courage.

Daring myself to write this book has shown me that courage is of a different order than my brown eyes. Courage is not in one's DNA. Courage is not an inborn predilection. Courage, once embraced, can't be expected to stick around. Courage has to be re-won, re-tested and re-earned every day in countless ways – many of them not yet envisioned or explored.

Each day I write, my companion, fear, sits by my side. Sometimes she even stops chattering and ceases telling me "You're a fool, you will leave this effort like those that came before"; "What you have to say isn't relevant, is redundant, is trite, is contrived, and is ugly". In that precious moment, when she actually goes quiet, I trust in myself. I embrace the notion that regardless of how this book is received, I have succeeded because I have given birth to a part of myself previously only experienced in previews.

So, to Jeff Goin's point, I don't have more courage, I have just learned to do it afraid.

"Limits like Fears are often just Illusion. What matters most is how well you walk through the fire."

—Charles Bukowski

All too frequently, I prefer illusion.

Illusions are obsessional.

I turn them around, look at them from all sides,
Investigate them from the back to the front.
I can nurture thoughts large and challenging.

I can fight the dragons in my mind. I can engage in a virtual heroic battle.

And, (secretly, best of all) I don't have to take in-life action yet manage to feel triumphant and heroic without ever having taken a risk or even left the comfort of my sofa.

Illusion is fictionalized reality.

Walking though fire is not for illusionists. Walking though fire dares the darkness, challenges the unknown, accompanied by a willingness to be humbled by the fire-walk. I can't be humbled by illusions – they are phantasmagorical, best suited to shadowboxing.

Walking into the fire of my fear demands that I become real. And, at the end, regardless of worldly outcome, becoming real is the ultimate triumph.

"The cave you fear
to enter
holds the treasures
you seek"

—Joseph Campbell

I have yet to meet someone who, if honest, does not acknowledge that they too, like me, have a cave that frightens at the same time that it beckons.

Do I run away, can I ever run away?

Can I hide my cave of unexplored darkness, the foreboding of dangers residing within?

Yet, what may those dangers actually be?

I actually don't think I am afraid of the not—so—pretty, unbleached inner me. I think most of us are more intimate with that aspect of ourselves than we care to admit.

My fear is that I may discover treasures, though they are coated in limestone and need to be excavated and hacked out of the cave walls.

Treasures that are not openly cascading from ancient trunks; inviting me to scoop them up and bring them into the light of day. Rather ones that require a flash lit walk along unexplored tunnels, a discerning eye to discover and identify them in the gloom and strength to bring them into the light.

And most frightening, once freed from their confinement, I will have to do something with them. I will have to carve out their beauty and polish them to shine.

I will have to be worthy of them.

Or, is it possible that I am more afraid of the disappointment I may feel if my treasures shine less brightly than I secretly believed?

"The great courageous act that we must all do, is to have the courage to step out of our history and past so that we can live our dreams."

—Oprah Winfrey

It is an enormous act of courage to "step out of our history and past" to live our dreams.

It is only by daring greatly that our truly authentic self, not the person we were told we should be, nor the one we are told that we are, nor the person we falsely believe we need to be, is embraced. The self that lies somewhere, often well camouflaged, who is continually praying that we find her before it's too late.

Your authentic self is not without blemishes, unfinished parts, and awkwardness. To be authentic is to have all these dents, dings and lack of cool, smooth perfection and celebrate your road tested self anyway. To be authentic is to embrace our perfect imperfection and see within it a glimmer of what is possible around the next bend.

We frequently tell ourselves that we have to "figure this part out; find out why" before we can move on. Holding on to "figuring it out" is a way of avoiding unavoidable change. Holding fast is a way of paying homage to the past that might not deserve such respect and loyalty. "Figuring it out" can be a way of giving away our power.

Authenticity has an energy to it that vibrates higher than anything else. At that moment, we get a taste of freedom; we feel joy, we feel found, as for the very first time. At that very moment, we often retreat and go back to our respective corners to "figure it out".

What good does it do you to keep open the door to a painful, conflicted, confused life story that is too small to provide joy? It's a waste of your life if you hold it too close.

"This being human is a guest house
every morning a new arrival.
A joy, a depression, a meanness,
some momentary awareness comes
as an unexpected visitor.
Welcome and entertain them all!
Even if they're a crowd of sorrows,
who violently sweep your house
empty of its furniture,
still, treat each guest honorably.
He may be clearing you out
for some new delight.
The dark thought, the shame, the malice,
meet them at the door laughing,
and invite them in.
Be grateful for whoever comes,
because each has been sent
as a guide from beyond."

—Rumi

The Guest House

To welcome with gratitude what comes unbidden, untidy, unwashed and unlikeable is the work of the second half of life. The young may experience much hardness, sorrow and disappointment, but there is a difference. To survive, they are called to don their armor and hold aloft their scythe, entering the field of battle to overcome, to triumph, to shout in defiance, "I am here and you can't destroy me!"

Arrival in middle age and beyond comes with an invitation to open welcoming arms to these undesirable, never vanquished guests. They live on in perpetuity. They are our essential partners if we yearn to lift the tarp that covers our soul and embrace, bow down to, and learn from this thing called life.

It takes the accumulation of being brought to our knees, of being humbled, of feeling lost in the midst of success, of gaining what we thought we desperately wanted only to discover that the emptiness inside remains, to accept that these forces are not only eternal, but essential to deepening our soul.

To fight them, to try and bar the door to entry is only to deepen a sense of disconnection from spirit. To be adrift from spirit is to become a stranger to our self; it is to succumb to fear of the very forces that can save us.

"**The world breaks everyone and afterward many are strong at the broken places.**"

—Ernest Hemingway

If we dare living in the reality that our hopes, beliefs, and self confidence can easily be broken by the world, we can become Kintsugi. Kintsugi is the traditional art of Japanese pottery that repairs ceramics with gold. Such repair makes the shattered object even stronger than the original.

Becoming broken is the work of the world.

There is not a one of us who does not suffer from a broken heart, a bent wing, or a bruised spirit. I think perhaps that is the purpose of living in the world, to test our boundaries, to learn new skills, to be broken so we can re-member, to greet the person we were sent here to become. Staying whole and unshattered means that we've never dared to leave the security of the shelf upon which we rest.

While I'm not sure I believe in God, I do believe that there is intelligence in the universe that can only develop and deepen itself through our experiences, battles and triumphs. We are the channel through which the universe expresses itself both its past, its present and most mysteriously, its future.

As we become stronger at the broken places we make our contribution to the evolution of humanity, the planet and the cosmos. We become players in the enormity of what surrounds us, we become alchemists who learn to take our baser selves and spin gold.

"Between stimulus and response,
there is a space.
In that space is our power
to choose our response.
In our response lies our growth and
our freedom."

—Viktor E. Frankl

That space is equal to the time between heartbeats, the seconds after our breath releases and before the next in-breath. This space is the place where potentiality lies.

To break the stuck-needle-on-the-vinyl record of repetitive experience, we must make a deliberate choice. To choose is to take responsibility for our actions, thoughts, and beliefs. To choose is to be emboldened, to become visible as well as to prepare for the possibility that we will make a "wrong" choice and embarrassment, perhaps humiliation may follow.

The outcome is without guarantees. However, you will have awakened your inner guidance and begun to ask "Is there a better way to respond? Is my immediate impulse one that will make me proud or shall I take a chance on an untried, but more present and authentic response?; Can I trust this new, tender voice that has emerged?"

So, it's up to you to decide how much freedom and growth you are ready for. Too much, too fast can be a formula for crashing and too little, too late can freeze you into inaction. It is a difficult balance, yet the opportunity is endlessly open to you. It's up to you if you choose.
The power to choose thrusts us into the center of our lives.

"TAKE EVERYTHING THAT'S BRIGHT AND BEAUTIFUL IN YOU AND INTRODUCE IT TO THE SHADOW SIDE OF YOURSELF. WHEN YOU ARE ABLE TO SAY, 'I AM MY SHADOW AS WELL AS MY LIGHT,' THE SHADOW'S POWER IS PUT IN SERVICE OF THE GOOD."

—Parker J. Palmer

"Living From the Inside Out." Naropa University 2015 Commencement address.

I am my shadow and my light; how could I not be? One cannot exist without the other. Every tree, animal, human casts its shadow. The brighter the light, the more defined the shadow. Do you judge the oak as flawed when it casts its shadow on a radiant summer day? Or do you, perhaps find joy, relief, and rest in its cast darkness?

We are desperate to only be viewed through the lens of our bright shiny selves and are terrified of being vilified, crucified for the corresponding shadow that co-exists. Society clamors for the starbursts as it simultaneously salivates for the inevitable fall from grace.

Why is that? Are we so frightened by the heart of our own darkness that we impale those outside ourselves as a way of proclaiming that we, I, am so perfect that I can cast boulders of judgment and derision upon another without fear of being stoned myself? However, it is precisely our disowned fear, our deeply unacknowledged shadows, our self-hatred that turns us into a builder of crosses for the coming crucifixions. The first person who is in need of my forgiveness is me. If I can't forgive myself I am incapable of forgiving you. If I can't tolerate my "less-ness", then I must destroy you for yours.

Failing to admit any dark undercurrents in our psyches we can become a raging, mindless mob yearning to be enraptured by the latest version of demagoguery that, for the moment, promises us our flawlessness, our chosen status, our guaranteed passport into heaven.

"To grow in love and service, you — I, all of us — must value ignorance as much as knowledge and failure as much as success … Clinging to what you already know and do well is the path to an unlived life. So, cultivate beginner's mind, walk straight into your not-knowing, and take the risk of failing and falling again and again, then getting up again and again to learn — that's the path to a life lived large, in service of love, truth, and justice."

—Parker J. Palmer

"Living From the Inside Out." Naropa University 2015 Commencement address.

As the world has become more automated, techno-animated, photoshopped, and roboticized, we appear to have fallen in love with the illusion and unkeepable promise that we can become inoculated against failure, fear, and broken-heartedness.

We become enraged (terrified) when someone suggests that we may be flawed or found wanting. We fear becoming last-year's model, outdated and junkyard bound.

We nip and tuck our soul's messy pursuit of self-discovery, we Botox our spirit's capacity for resilience. We show disdain for deepening into the wrinkles that proclaim hard fought battles in search of the Holy Grail – the holiness of finding ourselves.

Increasingly we appear to yearn for the exact slogan and newest jingle that will brand us, too, as a member of the tribe of the beautiful, smart and invincible. In such yearning there is no space for the messiness of failure or the humiliation of defeat. Yet, I continue to pray that I, you, we rediscover the power of being "reckless when it comes to affairs of the heart".

"… Since suffering as well as joy comes with being human, I urge you to remember this: violence is what happens when we don't know what else to do with our suffering."

—Parker J. Palmer

"Living From the Inside Out," Naropa University 2015 Commencement address.

> "Violence is what happens when we don't know what else to do with our suffering."

How have I not considered violence in this context before?

Violence and suffering are pandemic. Why are we not horrified by our universal suffering? Why do we have so little compassion for suffering, theirs and ours? Perhaps if we would come out from behind our emotional panic rooms we would confront suffering and actually feel at one with it.

We are all victims of violence whether we acknowledge it or not. When we see violence spread across the front page or in the evening news we breathe a sigh of relief. Violence is "out there," we are not its targets. But we are its victims. We are both the victim and the criminal. We have been exposed to so much suffering that we have built a force field to ward off its effects on us.

Until you are willing to acknowledge your suffering, your heartbreak, your pain; you will remain too afraid to identify with the suffering of others. When you are afraid to declare your suffering, you are liable to turn your violence, frustration, despair towards the "others". Screaming at your children is an act of violence. Being disrespectful and demeaning to a spouse is an act of violence. Humiliating an employee, a coworker, a waiter, anyone, is an act of violence. Feeling that hidden pleasure at someone else's suffering is violence.

We are all suffering. It's a matter of degree in how violence shows up in your life.

"Are you paralyzed with fear? That's a good sign. Fear is good. Like self-doubt, fear is an indicator. Fear tells us what we have to do. Remember our rule of thumb: the more scared we are of a work or calling, the more sure we can be that we have to do it."

—STEVEN PRESSFIELD, THE WAR OF ART

As one who has galloped away from a work or calling, I know the power that fear can exert. I have heedlessly rushed toward the uncertain and questionable in work or other pursuits and now realize that frequently those sprints were in the opposite direction of my calling, not a courageous running towards it.

Maybe I wasn't ready. I know that may sound like a cop-out, but I am not so sure. Looking over my shoulder at past endeavors, including a stint as a jewelry designer and creator of holiday greeting cards, I understand these as first steps to following the call to my creative spirit, putting a toe in creation's river and testing the currents.

Perhaps you are in the meandering stage. Perhaps you are playing around the edges of your soul's desire. No matter, your travels can change in an instant; your true destination can arise from behind the mist and you can step onto the yellow brick road with its unexpected poppy fields, screaming monkeys, and bad witches to be vanquished, yet it leads you to the Emerald Castle of wish fulfillment.

Finding our soul's work is not an enterprise for the faint of heart.

"Suffering is not holding you, you are holding suffering. When you become good at the art of letting yourself go, then you'll come to realize how unnecessary it was for you to drag those bundles around with you. You'll see that no one else other than you was responsible. The truth is that existence wants your life to be a festival."

—Osho

Some of us have a Ph.D. in Suffering. We savor it, like a rare delicacy, endlessly chewing it over, noting its variety of spices known by names such as humiliation, disregard, cruelty, abuse, shame and failure.

Suffering becomes our identity, a badge of curious and unlikely honor, a way of knowing ourselves and our place in the world. And, there can be quite a fight when challenged to let Suffering go.

Let go of it, for what?

What would be there to fill that gaping space?

Who would you be without your Suffering?

Many would feel abandoned when their Sorrow left the neighborhood: alone and identity-less, a shell of a person drained of a reservoir of endless ruminations, stories, and self-serving avoidance to discover their real selves. They would feel, perhaps for the first time, truly alone and naked in the world.

When we let go we really need to open up. When we release Suffering like a balloon into the sky, we are left with nothing in our empty hands.

Yet, those hands are now free to write, or paint, or dance or even to wave for help. Much can enter empty hands – water, nourishment, even another's hand willing to hold our own.

Holding on to Suffering's bundles keeps us from dancing with life's gifts.

It's time to dance. Life is offering you a festival.

"What's the smallest, tiniest thing that I can master and what's the scariest thing I can do in front of the smallest number of people that can teach me how to dance with the fear? Once we get good at that, we just realize that it's not fatal. And it's not intellectually real – we've lived something that wasn't fatal. And that idea is what's so key — because then you can do it a little bit more."

—Seth Godin

quoted by James Clear in jamesclear.com

Such a perfect question: "What's the smallest, tiniest thing that I can master and what's the scariest thing I can do in front of the smallest number of people that can teach me how to dance with the fear?"

Why don't we think about taking the tiniest step when we consider emerging from fear? I have never heard anyone think about this; they immediately think, "To overcome my fear I have to do something huge, public, perfect and…probably humiliating." It's that old defeatist, either-or proposition that stops us in our tracks. And, it should. If we haven't taken baby steps out into the stream, we sure aren't ready to swim in the ocean. I've used the same false belief to trammel my dreams. Then, I suddenly recognized that beneath that resides arrogance.

Is it hard to believe that arrogance can be a companion to the refusal to engage with the littlest thing to defeat fear? I think it often is. It's false pride peeking out behind the fear. False pride is an exaggerated conviction of our specialness, our unique awe-inspiring gifts. If I don't show up, I can't really fail, can I? If I don't show up, I won't be shocked at how much further I have to go or discover it was all a pipe dream.

So, maybe it is better to stay untested. At least then I can secretly nurse my specialness. However, I have discovered that it is not better; how can I discover who I really am and what I am made of or capable of becoming if I continue to live backstage?

"There are no true right or wrong decisions. All decisions contribute to your development and are an integral part of your evolving existence yet they are still separate from the self. A decision that does not result in its intended outcome is in no way an illustration of character. Still, it can have dire effects on our ability to trust ourselves and our self-esteem. You can avoid becoming your decisions by affirming that a "bad decision" was just an experience, and next time you can choose differently."

—Madisyn Taylor

Quoted in the DailyOM (www.dailyom.com)

I have recently made a decision to say "Yes" to offers, previously shrugged off, that come my way. I say "Yes" to social invites that before I would have hemmed and hawed about. I say "Yes" to online offers to put my writing online and see how it fares. I say "Yes" to myself when I want to visit friends in far away states and not use income as a roadblock.

Saying "Yes" is a way of defeating the "No's" protecting me from facing disappointment, anxiety, and failure. "Yes" is an affirmation that regardless of outcome I will benefit in some way, I will learn something that I didn't know before. "Yes" is building my courage muscle, enabling me to lift increasingly heavy weights of trial and error.

When you don't link the outcome of your efforts with your worth, adventures can ensue. Previously unseen paths hidden behind the brambles can be discovered and explored. Talents not perceived can take a cautious step out of the darkness.

Or, perhaps nothing of significance will happen at all. Perhaps it will fall to ash. While disappointing, it is not about my character. Each decision or action is part of the process of moving forward, of taking chances large or small, of showing up regardless of uncertainty, and that's where the value resides.

If I never take a chance, I rob myself of the ability to choose differently. And choosing differently may take me to places unforeseen.

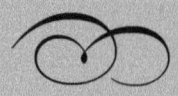

"...To have patience with everything unresolved in your heart and to try to love the questions themselves as if they were locked rooms or books written in a very foreign language. Don't search for the answers, which could not be given to you now, because you would not be able to live them. And the point is to live everything. Live the questions now. Perhaps then, someday far in the future, you will gradually, without even noticing it, live your way into the answer."

RAINER MARIA RILKE

LETTERS TO A YOUNG POET

We have arrived at the end of this journey. Perhaps I will pick up this journey again but then again, perhaps not.

This is my favorite quotation — one that reminds me that I will always have unresolved parts of myself. There will always be questions for which I have no answers, questions that I am not yet ready to have answered or to understand.

As I live the questions I hopefully will discover hidden parts of myself. Maybe never the whole picture, but that will have to be enough. That is enough.

Your Journey has molded you for your greater good, and it was exactly what it needed to be. Don't think that you've lost time. It took each and every situation you have encountered to bring you to the Now. And now is right on time."

ASHA TYSON

ABOUT LESLIE K. MALIN

Leslie considers herself to be a beginner at life, despite her many years in the world. No matter what she thinks she knows or has learned, she states that, "I am presented with my ignorance on a daily basis. And, that's just fine with me; well to be honest, sometimes it is quite unnerving and takes a while to digest! Whether it's working with clients, reading, being part of an online community, or having everyday conversations with friends and family, I discover wisdom that enriches my life."

Never leaving her creative leanings far behind, she has also been a jewelry designer, a partner in a holiday greeting card company that marries original art with meaningful quotations (www.EarthFriendlyGreetings.com), as well as continuing her writing and she most recently returned to painting.

A licensed Clinical Social Worker for over 35 years, Leslie has worked with thousands of people and families as a psychotherapist, Life Transition Coach, and a seminar leader for public groups, corporations, nonprofits and small business.

She was Clinical Director in a community mental health center on Long Island; a Senior Counselor for a boutique out placement firm in New York City working with management and executive level individuals as they navigated finding new employment, transitioning to entrepreneurship, moving into the nonprofit arena or even a fulfilling retirement. She was the Executive Director of Jewish Family Services of Ulster County, N.Y; she briefly ran a B&B in New Hampshire (a long held aspiration which was fun but less fun than being an actual guest), and had the privilege of counseling military personnel and their families at Fort Drum in Watertown, New York. Presently she maintains a private psychotherapy and coaching practice with offices in Kingston, New York.

Leslie is a graduate of Vassar College and holds a Masters in Social Work from Adelphi University School of Social Work.

Cracked Open is her first published book and the first in a series called *Reflections*. Have opinions that you want to share? Please leave reviews, we want to hear your voice.

To deepen your reading experience look for her companion journal, *Cracked Open, A Creative Journal for Personal Transformation*. This innovative journal is designed to assist readers in capturing their thoughts and feelings, tap into their creative and meditative energies and deepen their personal journey.

She is presently developing new online workshops and beginning her work on the second book in her *Reflections series: Forgiveness: A Gift You Give Yourself*.

You can connect with Leslie at www.LeslieMalinAuthor.com and email her at info@lesliemalinauthor.com.

Don't fail to sign up at www.JustThinkn.com to receive your special FREE eBook: *Life Happens. Happiness is a Decision.* Read her new blog posts, announcement of her new books, and workshop offerings, as well as special offers from other business partners she admires.

Join the conversation at her Facebook group at www.Facebook.com/LeslieMalinAuthor, or find her on Twitter at Leslie4Success and on LinkedIn.com/in/LeslieMalin. She says, "Together we can expand our knowledge, authenticity, awareness and connection. We need each other now, more than ever."

www.ingramcontent.com/pod-product-compliance
Lightning Source LLC
Chambersburg PA
CBHW040329300426
44113CB00020B/2697